The Team Success Handbook

12 Strategies For Highly Productive Entrepreneurial Teams

By Shannon Waller

Great teamwork is one of the most sought-after yet anguish-inducing qualities in the entrepreneurial universe.

Shannon Waller, one of the first members of our Unique Ability Team, has been expanding her contribution to Strategic Coach and our entrepreneurial clients and their teams for 20 years. Since 1995, she has been creating thinking structures, tools, and concepts that help entrepreneurial team members to be successful, valuable contributors in their companies. We are so happy that Shannon has captured much of her wisdom in this *Team Success Handbook*.

Thank you, Shannon, for your partnership, your commitment, and your Unique Ability. It has been transforming entrepreneurial teamwork for many, many years—our team included!

Babs and Dan

Printed in Toronto, Canada. May 2019. The Strategic Coach Inc., 33 Fraser Avenue, Suite 201, Toronto, Ontario, M6K 3J9.

This publication is meant to strengthen your common sense, not to substitute for it. It is also not a substitute for the advice of your doctor, lawyer, accountant, or any of your advisors, personal or professional.

Library and Archives Canada Cataloguing in Publication

Waller, Shannon, 1965-, author
        The team success handbook : 12 strategies for highly productive entrepreneurial teams / Shannon Waller.

Includes index.
ISBN: 978-1-64746-138-6 (Paperback)
ISBN: 978-1-64746-139-3 (Hardcover)
ISBN: 978-1-64746-140-9 (Ebook)
Library of Congress Control Number: 2020903016

        1. Teams in the workplace. 2. Success in business.
I. Title.

HD66.W37 2013   658.4'022   C2013-903182-0

Contents

To my Dad — editor extraordinaire.

I dearly wish you could have read this book.
Thank you for your undying love and support.

I miss you.

Introduction

In 1995, I started coaching the team members of entrepreneurial clients in The Strategic Coach® Program[1], a workshop program with phenomenal thinking structures, tools, and concepts to help successful entrepreneurs grow their companies. It reduces the complexity inherent in all businesses and increases the simplicity of how entrepreneurs handle their time, relationships (both personal and professional), money, and purpose.

As I was coaching our clients' team members, I realized that what I was trying to communicate to them wasn't getting through. There was a way of thinking that was getting in the way. Many team members who had worked for larger organizations were expecting the same type of management and structure in their entrepreneurial company, and it simply wasn't there.

I decided I needed to design a tool that would help people adopt an entrepreneurial attitude so they could better understand the person they were working for (usually the owner), and from there, develop strategies to help them be successful in an entrepreneurial company.

Together with my colleagues, I identified characteristics, ways of thinking, and actions that work in our company and our most successful clients' companies.

[1] For more information about The Strategic Coach® Program, please visit *strategiccoach.com*.

Out of that came The Entrepreneurial Attitude exercise[2], now a core tool in our Team Tools® workshops. The Entrepreneurial Attitude lists 12 different success strategies that we consider essential to be an effective, valued team member at Strategic Coach®. It's also what I've seen demonstrated by the most accomplished team members I've coached from other entrepreneurial organizations.

This handbook will give you, as an entrepreneurial team member, an in-depth understanding of each of these 12 strategies and how to use them to further increase your value to your organization and your sense of fulfillment in your work.

I can vouch for how effective these strategies are because they've worked for me. I joined Strategic Coach in 1991 as a sales assistant, and since then have progressed to being a salesperson, program designer, director, speaker, coach, and creator of the Strategic Coach® Team Programs using these tools. I'm thrilled to share them with you so you can grow as a person and as a professional, help grow your company, and fulfill your dreams.

To your success,

Shannon

2 See Appendix i

Preface
The difference between entrepreneurial teams and teams in other types of organizations.

Most of us work for or with some type of organization. They enable us to coordinate our talents with those of others to produce results. The type of results depends on the purpose of the organization. Those in healthcare differ from law firms, which differ from those in retail, which differ from government.

What's unique about entrepreneurial organizations versus what I would call more corporate or bureaucratic organizations can be summed up by certain values and characteristics.

Here's a chart to illustrate some of the differences:

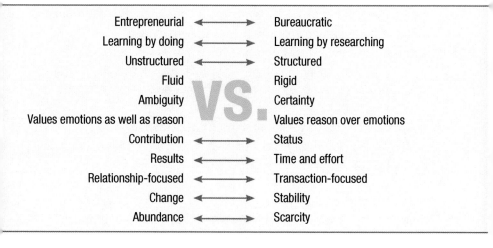

Entrepreneurial	⟷	Bureaucratic
Learning by doing	⟷	Learning by researching
Unstructured	⟷	Structured
Fluid		Rigid
Ambiguity		Certainty
Values emotions as well as reason		Values reason over emotions
Contribution	⟷	Status
Results	⟷	Time and effort
Relationship-focused	⟷	Transaction-focused
Change	⟷	Stability
Abundance	⟷	Scarcity

As you can see by looking at the left-hand column of the chart, it takes a certain mindset to be able to work in an entrepreneurial structure. There may not be any job descriptions, there may not be anyone there who's going to consistently manage you, and you'll be counted on to actively contribute and be engaged.

I've learned that there are some smart, lovely, and talented people who simply don't thrive in this environment. They need more structure and certainty in order to be really successful.

For others, like me, those other environments are too constraining and confining. I enjoy the fluid, evolving, constantly changing environment of an entrepreneurial organization. Not only do I enjoy it, I'm free to create more, contribute more, be rewarded more, and be constantly learning and evolving.

One of my burning desires in life, since I was a teenager, has been to know that what I was doing was making a difference. When I first went job hunting after university, with all the positions I looked at, I couldn't tell whether the work I was doing was actually making a difference for anyone. If I did the job, or someone else did, would anyone ever know or care?

Now I know that I was searching for a place where my Unique Ability® would be appreciated and valued. Isn't that what we all want and are searching for?

For me and for the team members I coach, this place we're searching for is within an entrepreneurial company that's growing, that appreciates peoples' unique talents and capabilities, and that is doing worthwhile work in the world.

If this is what you're looking for, this handbook will give you some of the key ways of maximizing your contribution and your rewards.

The definition of an entrepreneur.

What is an entrepreneur, and how is an entrepreneurial company different from a corporate structure?

Jean-Baptiste Say, an 18th-century French philosopher, defined an entrepreneur as someone who "shifts economic resources out of an area of lower and into an area of higher productivity and greater yield."

Merriam-Webster defines an entrepreneur as "one who organizes, manages, and assumes the risks of a business or enterprise."

Entrepreneurs are people who give up security in exchange for opportunity. Unlike most people who are content with a job, a regular paycheck, and clearly defined responsibilities, entrepreneurs are willing to jump into the unknown, betting on their intelligence, expertise, and ability to problem-solve and create solutions in the hopes of generating a profit.

Are they always successful? No. On average, four out of five new businesses fail. I like the response of Robert Kiyosaki, author of *Rich Dad Poor Dad*, who advises to fail faster so you can get to the fifth business as quickly as possible. Many entrepreneurs do just this, learning more from each deal, project, and relationship what works and what doesn't.

They trust more in their own experience than other people's, which makes them much more independent-minded. What does this have to do with a team member working for them? It means that you have to know they're not going to follow convention. They may not have attended business school, so they don't know or care how it's "supposed" to be done.

They're not interested in theory; they're interested in the practical realities.

They're leaders, not managers.

They find security in opportunity, not in someone else guaranteeing a paycheck.

They respect other people who have created their own success.

They're willing to invest in order to grow, and they're (usually) willing to be wrong—but they don't like it.

They start small, and test and experiment and refine as they go, rather than perfecting their product or service before it goes to market.

They feel strongly about things and often don't care to hide their feelings.

They're interested, committed, engaged people who respect others who are also interested, committed, and engaged.

Are they perfect? Absolutely not. Are they interesting? Oh yes!

Working for an entrepreneurial organization provides opportunities that aren't available in larger organizations. In smaller, more nimble organizations, you have an opportunity to make a real and lasting difference; to see, touch, and feel the results of your efforts; and to have far more responsibility much faster than you would following the corporate track.

At the same time, because things are so fluid, some of what people normally expect from employment, like job descriptions, regular reviews, and job titles, may not be there— unless you create them.

Like most successful working relationships, it's important to manage expectations:

- Don't expect to be managed—manage yourself, and manage up.
- Don't wait to be told what to do—figure out what you think needs doing, check in if you need to, and do it.
- Don't expect other people to always pat you on the back— learn how to motivate yourself and ask for positive feedback when you need it. (Yes, it still feels good.)

It takes a certain type of person, a more entrepreneurial type of person, to work for a less structured type of organization.

This handbook outlining the 12 strategies[3] to having an Entrepreneurial Attitude will give you the road map to make it the most fun, fulfilling, and rewarding experience of your working career.

3 See Appendix ii

Success Strategy #1: Create value.

Always work to provide leadership (direction), relationship (confidence), and creativity (capability).

Many team members think that they're hired strictly for what's on their résumé: their skills and their experience. Truthfully, though, there's so much more that you're going to be relied on for in an entrepreneurial organization. Your capabilities are really only one-third of the pie. Two other pieces are essential: providing direction and providing confidence.

Before I get to those, though, it's important to realize that value creation starts with your Unique Ability[4].

Your Unique Ability is what you do best and most love doing. It's found in those activities that give you energy rather than drain it, and where you sense that there's never-ending opportunity for growth.

Put another way, it's your passion—what you care about most. It's an area where you can be a hero to someone by creating value, and where there's a payoff or reward so you can keep growing your Unique Ability.

Leadership: providing direction.

How does a team member provide direction when it doesn't fall under their job title? Easy. It's part of an entrepreneurial culture for everyone—from the person who answers the phone, to a tech support person, to a project manager—to

---

4 For an in-depth discussion about Unique Ability and how to determine your own, please read the book *Unique Ability® 2.0: Discovery*.

Providing Capabilities
• Skills, knowledge, talents
• Specific tools
• Systems and processes

Providing Direction
• Eliminate dangers
• Focus opportunities
• Provide strategies and solutions

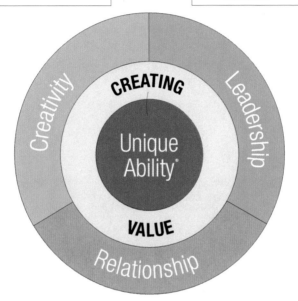

Providing Confidence
• Reinforce strengths
• Increase certainty
• Be a partner

provide direction and be a leader in their area of expertise.

One of our early team members, Julia, noticed that there weren't any coaching guidelines written for our associate coaches when they were learning to coach a workshop. They watched Dan Sullivan, the co-founder and lead coach of The Strategic Coach Program, and then delivered it themselves using the multimedia and materials. No prep notes, no coaching notes other than what they'd written down. Julia, as a former teacher and natural list maker, thought this was unusual, to say the least. After asking more about it and checking whether it was okay to write down the information, she created what is now the structure for the entire Strategic Coach Program. We have lists that describe what's in each workshop, coaching notes on all the concepts and tools, and timelines for how the days should flow. This was so useful that the other Strategic Coach co-founder, Babs Smith, Dan's wife and business partner, asked her to start and lead the Coach Resource Team. Dan no longer trains the coaches on the concepts and tools; the Coach Resource Team does.

By using her talents, paying attention to what was missing, and taking action, Julia created enormous value, which resulted in her being promoted to a leadership role.

Keep in mind that it's only ever appropriate to provide direction in an area that falls under your Unique Ability. Otherwise, it won't come across as credible. When you have superior skill and passion, you know what you're talking about, and people will listen.

Relationship: providing confidence.

Many people don't realize that entrepreneurial success is determined by confidence. It's our job as team members to give everyone we work with—owners, our teammates, vendors, clients, and customers—confidence about what we say and what we'll do.

Giving people confidence, so that they'll accept your leadership and capabilities, means providing certainty that they can count on you. Have you ever asked someone a question related to their job, and they replied, "I don't know," and stopped there? It's frustrating. My usual rejoinder is, "Will you please find out?" Giving other people confidence that you're actively engaged in finding a solution is vital if you're going to be a successful team member. It's perfectly appropriate to say, "I don't know right now, but I'll find out and let you know by the end of the day." Then, keep your commitment.

The person knows you're on the job and that you can be counted on. This confidence builds a strong sense of relationship that's crucial to teamwork.

Creativity: providing capabilities.

Your capabilities are the skills, knowledge, and expertise you bring to the organization, along with the technologies you've mastered. As mentioned, it's what's on your résumé. However, these really only provide value when applied creatively to achieving the goals of the business. When you create new systems, provide solutions, design layouts, organize files, listen really well to what a client needs, or hire a great new talent, you're providing capabilities.

Team members sometimes think that only the people who innovate and initiate new ideas are creative. That's one form of creativity, but certainly not the only one. If you're a great researcher, you're creative about how you gather and analyze information. If you're someone whose talent is organizing, you're creating new integrative systems that allow people to access what they need quickly and efficiently.

Providing leadership (direction), relationship (confidence), and creativity (capability) ensures that as an entrepreneurial team member, you are creating value at a high level.

Batteries included.

To be able to create value, you need to come to work fully engaged. We have an expression at Coach to describe someone with whom we want to work, especially team members. We say we want people with "batteries included."

Just like when you purchase a product that says, "batteries not included," it's very frustrating to hire someone who has the right qualifications and experience, dresses appropriately, and interviews well, only to have them put in a lackluster effort on the job. They have to be managed, checked up on, and cajoled into getting things done. It takes an inordinate amount of energy to be around them because they seem to have none of their own. No one on our team has time for that—we have our own work to focus on.

Alert, curious, responsive, and resourceful.
We hire people who have batteries included. They're alert
to what's going on around them, they're curious and always
want to learn more, they're responsive to the situation and
the people involved, and they're resourceful about obtaining
information, time, money, and creativity to solve the problem.
This is who you want to be and who you want on the team
with you.

People who have batteries included inspire confidence.
People with batteries not included don't.

 Take Action!
- Always be looking for how you can produce faster, easier, cheaper, and bigger results.
- Pay attention to those activities that give you energy versus those that don't. Make changes if you need to.
- Find new ways to be a leader, to provide confidence to others, and to be creative with your capabilities.
- Bring your own energy—have batteries included.

Success Strategy #2: Take initiative.
Look for ways to be proactive—solve problems, make improvements, and propose ideas.

Would you rather ask for permission or forgiveness?
So many team members I've worked with have brilliant insights and ideas that would help their company be more effective, but they're too fearful to mention them.

The usual reasons I hear are, "It's not my place," "I don't want to step on anyone's toes," "They won't like my idea," and "It's someone else's responsibility, and they'd resent it if I made a suggestion."

It drives me crazy.

Julian Simon, author of *The Ultimate Resource*, says, "There is only one natural resource on the planet: human ingenuity. It is only human ingenuity that makes everything else valuable."

If we hold back our ideas and insights, no one is learning anything. You're not learning whether your ideas have merit and how best to communicate them, and productivity and profitability are being compromised. What, really, do you have to lose?

If you're thoughtful, smart, polite, respectful, and clear, and set the context for your idea, the worst you'll get is a no. Live by the saying, "Ask for forgiveness, not permission."

One of our clients was telling me how much he wished his team members were willing to ask for forgiveness rather than permission. As far as he's concerned, always waiting for permission slows down the pace of the business, which he finds incredibly frustrating. He'd rather people take a moderate risk than never make a mistake. Most entrepreneurs know that a lot of their wisdom and experience came from making mistakes and learning what not to do, and appreciate the need to learn from doing.

Lewis Schiff, in his book *Business Brilliant*, has written an entire chapter on the value of failure and how successful entrepreneurs don't give up after failure like most people do. Instead, they learn from it and apply what they've learned to become more successful next time.

Most reasonable people are open to listening, even if they choose not to go with your idea. If you find that no one's willing to listen, then you may need to find a more open-minded, receptive company to work with.

Proactive vs. reactive.
Being proactive means stepping out, taking a risk, and trying something. It's a true entrepreneurial skill and capability.

Being reactive means being passive and waiting for others to go first. It means your actions are always being dictated by others rather than by your being proactive and creating something.

The most successful and valued people in our company don't avoid problems; instead, they actively look for them and tackle them head-on. They're not playing defense; they're playing offense.

Cathy is one of those people. As our lead program designer, she is constantly looking for ways to simplify the Program. She talks with all of our coaches and the client service team, and finds out what's not working so she can fix it. Cathy has a "puzzle brain"—she has a huge capacity to take many variables and make them all fit together elegantly and simply. The more complex the situation, the more she's in her element. She's always being proactive, suggesting improvements and making them, and very rarely needs to ask for forgiveness if it doesn't work out.

A natural "bossy boots—with love" kind of person, she's a wealth of creativity, support, and humor that makes our Program, and our company, better.

The more proactive she's been, the more valuable she's become. She does on her own what it used to take three people to do, as well as several other key tasks.

People are willing to give her that kind of responsibility because they know she's completely aligned with the company and committed to making it the best it can be.

She's so valuable that when her husband moved 1,500 miles away for a new position and she decided to follow him, we agreed there was no way she was leaving the company and worked out a solution for her to work remotely.

Having the confidence and drive to be proactive has been her formula for success at Strategic Coach.

 Take Action!
- Ask yourself, "How could this situation be improved? What could I do to make it better?"
- Start by taking small risks that have few negative consequences to acclimate yourself to taking risks.
- Recognize that asking for permission is a habit, and so is asking for forgiveness.
- Be sensitive to how your suggestions come across so people know you want to help make things better and aren't just being critical.

Success Strategy #3: Focus on results.

Focus on the bigger picture and the desired result, not just the time and effort required.

One of the most common complaints I hear from both team members and entrepreneurs is centered around this issue. It usually goes something like this:

Entrepreneur: "I'm so disappointed we didn't close this contract. It was vital to our success this quarter, and we blew it."

Team member: "But we put in so much time. We worked nights and two weekends, and put in a lot of effort putting everything together. Doesn't that count for anything?"

Entrepreneur: "Since we didn't get the contract, no!"

Both leave feeling hurt and misunderstood.

In truth, both are right. There was a lot of time and effort put in, and they didn't get the result.

What's vital for team members to know is that entrepreneurs live in the Results Economy, not the Time-and-Effort Economy.

In the Time-and-Effort Economy, you get a paycheck for putting in your time and presumably expending some effort.

When I was a cashier for a large grocery chain and punched a clock, it was abundantly clear that this was the economy I was in. It didn't matter if I was faster; the people who had been there longer got paid more—a lot more.

For entrepreneurs, there is no guaranteed income. They've crossed what we call the "Risk Line" into the Results Economy and rely solely on their creativity and ability to create value in order to get paid.

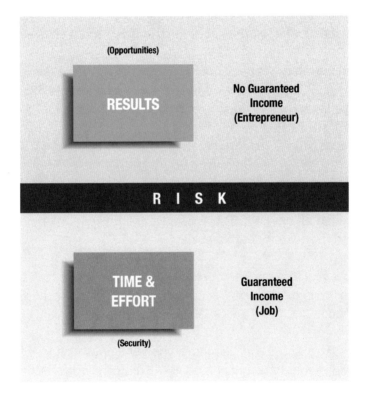

In the Results Economy, it's not about the security of having a job, but rather about the opportunities at stake. Sometimes, you put in the time and effort and don't get the result. Other times, you put in a little time and effort and get a big result.

The goal is to always be minimizing the time and effort while maximizing the results. Everyone in the company, regardless of their role, needs to know that, ultimately, they have to be focused on the results—of the company, of the project, of the quarter—in order to have the right perspective, even though they're likely paid a regular salary.

How do you find out what the desired results are?

Ask.

In the fast pace of day-to-day business, it's easy for others to assume that we think about and understand a project like they do. To see whether that's true, you need to ask.

Though it's common to think that everyone else approaches the situation the same way we do, the reality is that everyone has different background knowledge, skills, and problem-solving abilities, allowing them to contribute to the result in different ways using their unique strengths.

We use a number of different profiles to help identify people's strengths so we can be strategic about the talent we're bringing to a project. Kolbe[5] profiles identify how people

---

5 For more information about Kolbe and the Kolbe Index, visit *kolbe.com*.

strive and problem-solve. *StrengthsFinder 2.0* from The Gallup Organization identifies people's strengths. And the DISC[6] profile reveals people's personality types.

My favorite way of getting clarity on the desired result is to ask, "What does this look like when it's done and done well?"

Asking this question helps everyone get clear. Then you can work backward and determine everything that's in the way of producing that result. Too often, we start from the beginning with a goal and work through it without ever getting clear on our destination. Start with your destination, and you will immediately see how much effort is involved, the kind of time commitment you'll need to make, and the resources you'll need. Until you get clear on that, it's a guessing game.

 Take Action!
- Find out your Kolbe* MO at *www.kolbe.com* and share it with your team.
- Get your CliftonStrengths[†] profile (available in the books *Strengths-Based Leadership* by Barry Conchie and Tom Rath and *StrengthsFinder 2.0* by Tom Rath).
- If you want to know more about your personality and how that impacts your approach, go to the Personality Insights website and do your DISC profile.
- Always ask, "What does this look like when it's done and done well?"

6 For more information about the DISC profile, visit *personality-insights.com.*

Success Strategy #4: Have an ownership attitude.

Take full responsibility for your projects, your communication, and your actions.

Responsibility = Blame?

"Taking responsibility" is such an interesting phrase. Most people interpret it to mean "taking the blame." Blame is even the first synonym that comes up in the Microsoft Word thesaurus.

While it certainly includes admitting when you've made a mistake and setting it right, it also means taking the credit when you've done something well. It means owning something and making it yours—both the good and the bad.

Responsible means "able to respond." If we're not taking ownership for our actions, behaviors, and communication, then we're powerless to change them or make them better.

One of my least favorite sayings is, "It's not my job." I want to say, "Really? Is the success of your company important to you? Then it's your job."

The best team members take responsibility for the experience the company is creating. Even if it's not part of their day-to-day activities, they know that it's important and find a way to make the right thing happen, usually by engaging other team members to help solve the problem.

This broader perspective is vital. As I've already talked about, not everything is defined, predictable, and consistent in an entrepreneurial company. Unexpected things are going to come up, and the whole team needs to be ready and able to respond.

I know I've grown the most when I've had a project that did not turn out to be completely successful. When I learned from it and applied what I'd learned to the next situation, I became more successful. However, in those instances where I didn't take responsibility, when I didn't "own" my part in it and got defensive and felt like a victim, I didn't learn anything. All I figured out was how to avoid that situation in the future, which dramatically restricted my opportunities.

I tell people all the time that if we want to grow professionally, we need to be prepared to grow personally too.

While the purpose of this handbook is to help you at work, much of it will also help you grow as a person outside of work. You'll find that your personal relationships will strengthen, your ability to accomplish your personal goals will expand, and you'll become a happier and more successful person, not just a successful team member.

Although much of management theory makes a distinction between our personal and professional selves, I've noticed that we all take ourselves home at night. In reality, we're one person in many different environments and situations. Although some environments bring out the best in us more than others do, the more integrated we are, the healthier, happier, and more successful we'll be.

Learning organizations.

The best entrepreneurial companies have a high tolerance for risk and for making mistakes. Sit down with any business owner and ask how they learned what they know. They'll tell you all about the mistakes they've made—all the times they said the wrong thing, misunderstood what a client wanted, didn't appreciate how crucial a deadline was, or lost a valued employee because they didn't let the person know how important they were.

Even those entrepreneurs who are somewhat risk-averse accept the need to try things, experiment, start small, and learn before they launch a brand-new initiative. They'll do everything they need to do to minimize and mitigate the risk, and then they go and do it. Regardless of the outcome, they then focus on what they could do better next time.

Our greatest lessons occur not when things go as expected, but when they don't, and we learn what to do differently next time.

Entrepreneurial team members always need to be learning too. If you never take a risk, if you never make a mistake, you're playing it safe. You can do all the research you want, but at some point, you have to take action and learn from what happens.

Trust.

Part of taking greater responsibility and ownership is building trust with your team and your entrepreneur.

I've been coaching entrepreneurial team members since 1995, and neither Dan nor Babs has ever seen me coach a workshop. That's an incredible amount of trust to give someone, but they did, and continue to do so. We were aligned on the result, and they know how aligned I am with them and the company, and so I have a lot of room to both succeed and fail.

There's something interesting about trust. When it's given, you work really, really hard to be worthy of it.

Some entrepreneurs trust their team because they don't have the mental energy or interest to manage them closely. Others do it because they know it brings out the best in people.

You can encourage your entrepreneur to trust you by not making assumptions. Instead, ask, "What do I need to know in order for this project to be a success?"

Find out what they're worried about so you can protect against it. Ask, "What's the worst-case scenario? What are you worried about, so I can take steps to make sure that doesn't happen?"

Then ask, "What's the best-case scenario? What do I need to be working toward?"

And, finally, ask, "What's your criteria for success? What standards do I have to make sure I hit for you to have confidence?"

After the project is complete, take the time (usually not more than 20 minutes) to reflect on the experience and figure out what worked, what didn't, and what you'd do differently next time. Share this with your entrepreneur, and they'll be impressed with how closely your thinking process matches theirs.

Take Action!

Ask the following questions before starting a project so you're taking ownership over the process and the result:

- "What do I need to know in order for this project to be a success?"
- "What's the worst-case scenario? What are you worried about, so I can take steps to make sure that doesn't happen?"
- "What's the best-case scenario? What do I need to be working toward?"
- "What's your criteria for success? What standards do I have to make sure I hit for you to have confidence?"

Success Strategy #5: Be in alignment.

Find out the overall goal or desired result, and do what you need to do to align with it.

Alignment can be subtle, but it's extraordinarily important.

Align on values.

One thing that's vitally important to appreciate is that businesses run by entrepreneurs are generally for-profit businesses. While this may seem obvious, I managed to hire not one but two people whose goal was to work for a non-profit organization. Essentially, our business model wasn't one they were aligned with, and both left after a short time.

Ignoring this key factor or thinking it won't matter doesn't work. Work engages your whole self, not just your head, and if the purpose behind the work you're doing doesn't resonate with you, you'll never engage all your capabilities or experience the success you're looking for.

Alignment, ultimately, is about values. It doesn't mean that you don't get to have your opinion about how things are being done, but it does mean that the work you're doing, and the work the company does, is meaningful to you. If it's not, it's hard to get excited, stay the course, or be creative.

I find entrepreneurial companies more demanding, in a good way, than corporate or bureaucratic organizations. They require that you care (your heart), that you think (your head), and that you act (your gut). They require your whole self. I'm fortunate to have found a company that aligns with my personal values and whose values align with mine.

At Strategic Coach, we work for a husband-and-wife team (Dan Sullivan and Babs Smith). In many companies, this is a recipe for disaster. Rarely are couples 100 percent aligned, and the consequences are felt throughout the team as people take sides, build factions, and lobby for resources.

Dan and Babs knew they needed to stay aligned as their company and success grew, so they came up with their personal "Prime Directives." These three Prime Directives are the checkpoints against which they evaluate all their key decisions. They're very different people, and these three ground rules keep them aligned:

1. We won't do anything that would negatively impact our teamwork and intimacy.
2. We will always maintain control over the forces of our growth.
3. We align only with people who are aligned with us.

On the subject of values, one of my favorite clients to work with, The Hotze Group based in Katy, Texas, is extremely clear on the importance of their core values and of their team being in alignment with them. A statement of these principles is printed on a card that everyone carries with them, and the Leadership Team recites it (from memory) at every leadership and company meeting. While it's quite lengthy, it boils down to "We're committed to helping people obtain and maintain health and wellness naturally." It guides their decisions, actions, alliances, research, and who they hire.

Do you know your company's values? Do they mesh with yours? Are you aligned with the overall goals of the company and the difference it makes in the marketplace? These are vital questions to ask and keep asking so you know what you're working toward. Often, asking these questions helps other people get clear, so persevere until it makes sense to you.

Align on the result.

The other place to make sure you're aligned is on the specific results you're working to achieve. Do you know what you're aiming for—what it looks and feels like when it's done well? Remember the old joke, "To assume makes an ass out of u and me"? Well, it's true. More conflict, misunderstandings, hurt feelings, and under-performance are a result of assumptions than almost anything else.

While basic assumptions can be accurate, too often we assume that other people will approach problems the same way we do, will have the same sense of timing, and are working toward the same result. Well, we're wrong.

We're all unique in our approaches. One of the reasons I appreciate psychometric profiles like Kolbe, DISC, CliftonStrengths, and Myers-Briggs is that they put language to people's behavior. It's extremely powerful to know how someone strives and solves problems (Kolbe), what some-one's personality is like (DISC, Myers-Briggs), and where someone's strengths lie (CliftonStrengths). All of a sudden, you know what you can count on that person for. You know how they're similar and how they're different from you, and you can use that knowledge to play to each of your strengths and get freed up from doing things you don't like. You no longer assume—you know.

One of my very favorite people to work with at Coach is Ele-onora. Besides being a lovely person, she's an exceptional event planner. In terms of our Kolbe profiles, we could not be more different. She's detail-oriented and follows through on everything, whereas I'm at my best creating new things where there's no plan or certainty. Together, we're a fabulous team. She loves doing the things I don't, and I'm freed up to do what I do best and that she doesn't enjoy.

What makes our teamwork really sing is that we're both clear and aligned on the result we're trying to produce, which is usually a team event for a client. Without a common goal that was really clearly spelled out, we'd just annoy each other. Getting aligned on the specific result of a project, for instance, is what allows everyone to contribute their best tal-ents to accomplish it.

What's the definition of a result? Again, mine is the answer to the question, "What does it look like when it's done and done well?" Spending time describing it, getting specific, adding the details—including the time frame, budget, and quality standard—makes all the difference to people's understanding. It's very different to say, "We're going to build a house" than "We're going to build a three-bedroom, two-bathroom, 2,100 sq. ft. house downtown with top quality finishings for maximum $200/sq. ft. in six months." It isn't until you start getting detailed that people can really put their best talents to work. I'm not naturally a detailed person, but I've learned that my projects never turn out the way I want them to unless I'm extremely clear on what they look like when they're done and done well.

 Take Action!
- Learn your company values. If they're not stated, write down what you think they are.
- Check out Zappos.com for a great set of values to inspire you: *zapposinsights.com/about/core-values*
- Always get specific about the results you're shooting for, and don't hesitate to ask the "dumb" questions. Someone else is likely wondering the same thing.

Success Strategy #6: Be a partner.

Value and respect others' talents and goals as well as your own.

If I could get only one message across to team members, it would be to be your entrepreneur's partner.

While it may be your entrepreneur's signature on your paycheck, you are a vital partner in the success of the business. What you do, or don't do, impacts the company. If you treat your contribution as important, others will too.

A synonym for partner is collaborator, and that's who you are. When you value others' talents and goals as well as your own, it gives you a clearer perspective on how you can contribute.

Beyond the job description.

I'm not a big fan of traditional job descriptions. They describe what you're supposed to do, but not how well, and they leave out the results you'll be accountable for, which is the most important thing to know.

Although there is always some hierarchy in all companies, in entrepreneurial companies, status is based on creativity and contribution, not on job titles.

For example, let's say you were hired to be the receptionist (or, as I prefer, the Director of First Impressions). You could either see this as an entry-level position to get out of as soon as possible, or you could take the role seriously and give it your best. If you think about it, every phone call is an opportunity to help the company be more successful. If you handle the calls quickly and with a smile in your voice, you'll make a great impression on existing and potential clients. They'll be impressed that your organization has found someone so capable to be on the front desk. As the company grows, so will your opportunities.

In addition, you'll likely see some areas of the company that need to be improved. If the same person calls back five times about the same issue, you can flag it to the team or team leader that the problem isn't getting solved, and a new system will need to be put in place. And depending on the volume of calls and appointments, you probably have some free time during which you can take on other projects.

If you're proactive, capable, and engaged, and if the company is growing, you'll undoubtedly be asked to take on even more responsibility. If you're great with people, you could move into sales or customer service. If you're great with systems, perhaps you'll have a role in managing the office. Then you'd have a choice to make about whether you want to change roles, but you may be having too much fun where you are.

However, if you don't act like a partner, aren't proactive, and just do a merely competent job versus a stellar job, you won't be given any opportunities. You'll be in the same role, frustrated, likely bored, and complaining about the lack of opportunity.

Speak up.

Too many times, I've had conversations with team members in which they mentioned some very real concerns about potential issues, but were afraid to share them. They were concerned that it wasn't their place, even though not sharing them would mean their entrepreneur would be put in a compromising position. Not good!

We all have our blind spots, and entrepreneurs are no exception.

My coaching is always, always to speak up. The other person may or may not listen, but you've been their partner by not staying silent.

I'm a huge fan of Susan Scott and her book *Fierce Conversations*. What I find so useful is her structure for having what can be difficult conversations in ways that are authentic, that get to the heart of the matter, and that build rather than destroy the relationship.

Most of us avoid confrontation because we're scared that bringing up uncomfortable topics will upset the relationship. We're not confident in our ability to have these deeper, more challenging conversations.

However, there's a cost to only being nice, to keeping it light. We never get deeper with people, we never know what really matters, and we're hamstrung to deal with issues that are getting in the way.

If you've found yourself aware of a problem but reluctant to bring it up because you don't feel it's your "place," then you've fallen into this trap.

There are effective and ineffective ways to communicate. One of the best ways to communicate is through questions. Instead of launching into all the potential dangers you see, simply ask a few key questions, for example, "If this new project is a raving success, how do you think we could handle the additional need for technicians?"

Or perhaps you have knowledge about a client that your entrepreneur doesn't that suggests their usual approach won't land appropriately. You could say, "Joe, are you aware that the new investment the client made didn't work out and they're not feeling at all confident about their financial situation right now?"

The usual response is, "No, and thank you for telling me." Occasionally, you won't get as warm a reception, but don't let that stop you from giving a "heads-up."

You have an enormous amount to contribute—unique skills, passions, talents, and ways of looking at things that other people don't. You may not always be right, but holding yourself back is the greater danger.

Take Action!

- Phrase your concerns in a genuine way as questions. Be open to a conversation.
- Regardless of your current role in the organization, focus on the contribution you're making, not your status or lack of it. All the status you'll ever need will come as a result of your contribution.

Success Strategy #7: Take action.

Whenever possible, make things happen. Don't wait for others to make the first move.

Although similar to the second Success Strategy, take initiative, this strategy is actually a little bit different.

Taking action is about getting into motion, not waiting until all the *i*'s are dotted and the *t*'s are crossed. You see, all learning comes from doing, not thinking about doing. It isn't until you start doing something that you get feedback from the world—your clients, customers, teammates, and so on— on whether what you're doing is creating value for them.

Taking a small step and learning from it is infinitely better than taking no steps.

People don't realize that they're always in a creative relationship with the world. We have our say, and it has its say. The longer we just think about what we're going to do, mull it over, and go do more research, the more we get attached to our own way of thinking. It makes it harder to learn from our experience and adapt our offerings.

A far more collaborative process is to do something, see what happens, figure out what worked and what didn't, and then do it again, incorporating what you've learned.

It's this process of thinking, doing, and learning that is the hallmark of all successful entrepreneurs. Like good marketers, they're always testing, testing, testing, and never assuming they know what will work until it's been proven in the marketplace.

One practical action that works is worth all the theories in the world.

Avoid the perfectionism trap!

If you find that you're delaying or second-guessing yourself, you may be falling into the trap of perfectionism and procrastination.

The question I ask myself when I'm in danger of getting perfectionistic is, "Will it work?" Getting something to the point where it works, rather than being perfect, is the standard I need to hit. Is this handbook perfect? Undoubtedly not. Does it get the point across? My early readers tell me it does. Great. Now I can get it out to a larger audience, continue to get feedback, and use that coaching to enhance future versions.

The cost of not doing something is almost always higher than the cost of putting something out that's good, but not perfect.

Take Action!
- Start small, take a step, and see what happens. Learn what you could do better next time.
- Read *One Small Step Can Change Your Life: The Kaizen Way* by Robert Maurer, Ph.D.

Success Strategy #8: Be open.

Be receptive to new ideas and initiatives. Prepare and plan for change.

Staying open to new ideas can be a challenge. We often get comfortable with our own way of thinking and doing things. It takes courage and a willingness to get out of our comfort zone to entertain a different approach.

A trait of successful entrepreneurs and team members. What impresses me about entrepreneurs, at least the best ones, is how open they are. They're constantly willing to grow and to move past old ways of thinking to new, more successful approaches.

The clients who are most successful in the Coach Program are the ones who are open to the thinking processes of our tools and concepts. Our tools provide the framework, and the content is all theirs. We know they have the answers they need if they can simply eliminate all the clutter so they can do their best thinking.

The same is true of team members. Those who are able to look at a situation from another person's perspective, who can let go of limiting beliefs, and who are receptive to different approaches are the ones who are the most successful.

There is little that's static in a growing entrepreneurial company. It requires constantly adapting to new and changing circumstances. If you see this as being exciting and interesting, you'll have no trouble keeping pace. If you look at changes as interruptions and the wrong way of doing things, then life in an entrepreneurial company will be difficult.

Prepare and plan for change.

Kolbe has some great coaching for people who naturally create and follow systems and who don't change things without a lot of justification. It's to "prepare and plan for change."

I love that advice because it means that you can use your talents to carefully observe the patterns of your business, predict what the changes might be, and prepare for them.

Paul is an extremely capable and talented project manager at Strategic Coach. He manages all of Dan's production projects and is also our head of marketing.

Dan often praises Paul's ability to look into the future—what he calls "high beams"—and come up with alternatives. Dan frequently changes the plans, spontaneously writing a book or coming up with a new idea versus what was on the schedule. Paul always has plan B, C, and D at the ready, having strategically figured out what is most important and where there is flexibility in the schedule. Quite often, he'll build in extra time in case certain projects take longer than expected. Does he always tell Dan? No—only if he needs to. Paul epitomizes "prepare and plan for change," and it's been a core part of his success at the company.

When I'm coaching, I'll often ask people to track their time for two to three weeks, and then start to predict when they will have time to focus on key projects and to schedule regular planning time. Having control of your time is a necessary prerequisite for feeling confident and in control of your life.

Quite often, I get the response, "But there's no predictability to my day; it's always changing." Yes, that's true. But, if you step back far enough, you'll be able to discern a pattern. Why? Because people have patterns. Even the most erratic, Attention Deficit Disorder person you work with has a pattern. They're either a morning person, or not. When they're in the office, you can likely predict when they're going to need you, and when they won't. You can also likely predict the type of questions they'll ask you. If you've worked with someone for years and are still being surprised, then you probably haven't been paying attention!

Even customer calls have patterns. If you're someone who handles client calls, track the volume for a few weeks. You'll likely notice that you get a surge of calls first thing, and then it likely eases up until after lunch. Use the lull to work on other projects, focus on new improvements, or learn a new capability.

 Take Action!
- Be willing to go outside your comfort zone to consider new ideas and opportunities.
- Pay attention to patterns of activities, calls, and so on to be able to anticipate what's coming next.

Success Strategy #9: Communicate.

Learn how others like to communicate. Close "open files" — let people know when tasks are done and what happened.

Communication is the response you get (not necessarily what you intended).

I love this definition of communication because it places the responsibility on you, the communicator, not on the receiver.

Far too often, I hear the following complaints from entrepreneurs and team members.

The misunderstandings can be about the content:
- "She just jumped into the middle of the story without giving me any context. It took me forever to figure out what she wanted."

or
- "He went on and on. Why couldn't he just get to the bottom line?"

Or, it's about how it's given, for example:
- "She's been giving me dribs and drabs of information about this project for weeks. How am I supposed to make sense of it all?"
- "Why did he put that in an email when it was a top priority? Why didn't he call me or come and get me?"

Or the timing:
- "Why does he give me things to do in the morning? Why can't he do it the night before when I'm planning for the next day?"
- "Why does she interrupt me all day? It takes me forever to find out where I was!"
- "Can't he see I'm busy? Is he oblivious?"

Or all of the above.

We've designed an exercise called The Communication Builder (see Appendix) to get at the key but often overlooked elements of communication. Here are the essential parts of this thinking tool.

1. How we like to give information.
How we like to give information has a lot to do with how much mental energy we have for certain types of activities. The best measure of this, by far, is the Kolbe profile. For example, one of the Kolbe striving instincts is Fact Finder*, which is how we gather and share information. On a scale of 1 to 10, I'm a 3. Now, before you think this is a weakness, the advantage of a 3 in Fact Finder is that I simplify. I can take large amounts of information and discern quickly what's most important, and not get caught up in "analysis paralysis."

I work with a number of people who are an 8 in Fact Finder. I can count on them to dig deep, get all the details, and be very thorough. Do they ocasionally get lost in the details?

Yes, which is when they can come to me. I can't help them research, but I can help discern what's most important.

For communication, it means I want the essentials. If I were your client and you were giving me a report, it would be vital to put the conclusions in the Executive Summary at the very beginning. I may never look at the back-up research, but I like knowing that you did it.

2. How we like to receive information (and it may not be the same as how we like to give it).
I strongly dislike receiving voicemails, especially detailed ones. I find them time-consuming because it means I have to listen carefully and write things down. I'd rather just get an email.

But guess what? I love leaving voicemails. Why? Because it's the closest I can get to being face to face or being on the phone. Voicemail captures my energy, my tone, and is much richer than just sending an email full of emoticons. Ironic, isn't it?

If we assume that everyone likes to receive information the way we do, we're in trouble. It's worth doing this exercise with your teammates (and spouse) to learn what works best for them. Hint: You'll know you're overwhelming them when their eyes glaze over.

3. The best time and worst time to communicate with us.
Some of us are morning people, and some aren't. Some of us find interruptions energizing and a welcome break, while others find them incredibly distracting and time-consuming.

Generally, I love interruptions, except when I'm focusing to make a deadline. That's when I'm at my most creative, so it's important for people to know that.

My colleague with whom I used to share an office two days a week loathes interruptions. This was perfectly illustrated one day when our marketing director opened the door, stuck his head in, and asked if he could interrupt. Simultaneously, I said, "Yes" and she said, "No."

4. What we need when we're stressed.
Our ability to effectively communicate changes when we're stressed. We tend to support other people the way we ourselves want to be supported.

This came to light in one teamwork workshop that both the entrepreneur and a key team member attended. After completing The Communication Builder, he stated that what he needed was time alone to focus. What she needed was to talk it through and have reassurance.

Here's how it played out: When he saw she was stressed, he would leave her alone, and she felt neglected and uncared for. When she knew he was stressed, she'd be in his office talking and offering reassurance, leaving him feeling harassed and annoyed.

Neither of them felt at all supported. After doing the exercise, they realized that they'd each been giving the other person what they themselves needed, and committed to switching it around.

You may already have figured a lot of this out. But we can always get better. Think through The Communication Builder[7] for yourself—it only takes about five minutes—and share it with those you communicate with most often. You'll find out what you're already doing that works, and undoubtedly identify a few improvement ideas too.

Close open files.

A huge waste of time and mental energy for both team members and entrepreneurs comes from not closing what we call "open files."

An open file is anything you've asked someone to do, but don't know the result of yet. For entrepreneurs, it's often not knowing where a document is, or the status of a project, or the result of a client interaction.

For team members, it's not knowing the action items from a meeting, whether the priorities have changed, or what follow-up is needed for a client.

For some people, especially those with a long Follow Thru* on the Kolbe profile, even asking them if the task is done is somewhat insulting. Don't you know they can't sleep at night if an item on their to-do list isn't done? They assume you don't trust them when that's not the situation at all. If they weren't trusted, you wouldn't have asked them to do it in the first place.

Others of us appreciate the reminder and don't consider it nagging at all.

---

7 See Appendix iii

The Open-File Syndrome

What I've learned is that it's not a trust issue, it's a communication issue, and it's important for everyone to close the communication loop.

Otherwise, someone's left wondering, "Is it done yet? What happened?" When are they thinking this? In the car when they've forgotten their cell phone, in the shower when it's inappropriate to call, or at 3 a.m. when they can't sleep—as illustrated on the previous page.

Depending on how someone answers the questions in The Communication Builder, you'll know how much information they need and when they need it.

We can save each other a lot of mental energy and stress by taking a few moments to send a quick email, to leave a note on a desk with the item checked off, to give a brief update in the hallway, or even to send a text. It's incredibly reassuring to know when something's done, and by closing the communication loop, we free up their thinking for more productive pursuits.

Take Action!
- Do The Communication Builder with your entrepreneur, your teammates, and your family.
- Close open files in the way that makes the most sense for the other person.
- Don't assume everyone communicates the same way you do. Learn what works for them and for you.
- Pay attention to when people's eyes glaze over—they've had enough!

Success Strategy #10: Learn how to handle strong emotions.

Have confidence and stay calm when dealing with emotionally-charged situations. These are a normal part of entrepreneurial life.

I appreciate when entrepreneurs are open about their successes and failures, what they're excited about, and what they're upset about. It makes it so much easier to know what's going on. Pretty much, what you see is what you get.

It means you don't have to play a guessing game about what they're feeling. It's not hidden behind "politics" and game playing.

Having said that, it can be a little more intense than what you're used to. For me, once I understood that the owners were being real, it gave me a lot more appreciation and the capacity to deal with the strong emotions in the office.

When a sale gets made, a deal gets closed, or a problem gets solved, there's a lot of excitement and often a celebration. Expect high fives, going out for lunch, and the occasional bonus.

On the flip side, when things aren't going well, you'll see anger, frustration, sadness, and even sometimes tears.

Babs, in the early days of the company, would often get emotional when she felt strongly about something. Business owners crying? Yes! They're people too, and as she grew more confident in her capabilities and those of the team, the tears went away. I feel privileged to know her as a person with feelings.

Far too many team members treat the business owner as a role, and not like a real live human being with feelings. Those of us who have close relationships with Dan and Babs know how to work with their strong emotions, and we know that we can also be our true selves. It leads to an honesty and authenticity that I think is unusual in most companies.

Hopefully, the business owner or team leader you work with isn't on an emotional rollercoaster. Working with someone who's up in the clouds one day and down in the dumps the next is challenging.

To some extent, though, it comes with the territory when owning a business. As an owner, they feel things deeply. Successes and failures really impact them. And, they carry a huge responsibility running the business (they are on the hook for making sure bills are paid and payroll is met), something that team members don't always grasp and respect.

Business is inherently risky, and it's why we work hard with our entrepreneurial clients to make sure they're always protecting their own confidence so they can manage that risk with clarity and self-assurance. We start every workshop with a Positive Focus® exercise[8] that asks them about their five biggest areas of progress, both personally and professionally, over the last 90 days. It's essential that we do this. If we don't, it's easy for people to focus on what didn't happen, where they're falling short of their ideals, and problems they don't know how to solve. It doesn't matter how much money they're making—they often come in with this mindset.

You can do this too. Knowing that your entrepreneur is likely focusing on the negatives, say to them, "I know there are some urgent problems to solve, but let's look back for a moment and see how much progress we've already made."

As soon as you do this, it puts everything back into perspective. It's not that the problems have gone away, it's just that now you're bringing them to a more positive, confident mindset.

It's well documented that strong fear is anathema to creativity. When we're panicked, we're in "fight, flight, or freeze" mode and not accessing our higher level problem-solving capabilities.

Whose emotions do you need to manage?

When I was coaching this exercise in a workshop, a client made a really interesting point. She said, "It's not my entrepreneur's strong emotions I have to worry about; it's my own."

I was struck—it had never occurred to me. But of course we have strong responses to situations. How we handle them, and ourselves, often determines our success.

8 See Appendix iv

Do you have strong responses, both positive and negative? Are you putting yourself on a rollercoaster?

If so, do the Positive Focus exercise for yourself too. Or try an exercise that Dan does: Every night, write down your three wins for the day and what you want your three wins to be for tomorrow. I've been doing this quite consistently, and it's profound how such a simple exercise keeps me grounded and focused on what's working instead of what isn't, despite some very challenging days.

I've learned that even on a bad day, not everything was bad. There's always something that went well, something worth acknowledging and celebrating. However, if I paid attention only to the negative things, then I'd feel down and depressed, with little or no mental energy with which to make things better. Focusing on the positive gives me confidence to deal with things that aren't as I'd like them to be.

Always, always protect and reinforce your confidence and the confidence of those around you.

 Take Action!
- Do The Positive Focus for yourself at the beginning of meetings, with other team members, with your entrepreneur, and even with clients.
- Manage your own emotions: Take a walk, breathe, pause—whatever you need to do to get back under control.

- Don't take it personally: It's these strong emotions that drove the growth of the business in the first place. In many cases, they are just looking for someone to take action, not someone to blame.

Success Strategy #11: Have patience and compassion.

Look at the situation from the other person's point of view. Recognize that it takes time to change habits.

As we've talked about in the previous strategies, we all bring different perspectives and talents to bear in any situation. The ability to step out of our own perspective and see things from another's point of view is not easy, especially if the other person is angry or upset. The most natural response is to get defensive or upset yourself.

However, this isn't going to move the situation or the relationship forward. Until we can truly see things from the other person's point of view, we won't know how to bridge their thinking with our own. You only have half the story—yours.

Dr. Barry Johnson, in his brilliant book, *Polarity Management: Identifying and Managing Unsolvable Problems*, discusses how people polarize, and how instead of championing our own opinion, we first need to meet people where they are.

In Strategic Coach, we coach clients on how to have an in-depth conversation about the other person's goals, fears, opportunities, and strengths before they do any business together. It isn't until we know where someone wants to go that we can help them get there.

Often, once we know the whole story, we have much more compassion for where they are and how they got there, and we see what actions are necessary to bridge the gap.

I had a big wake-up call with one of my colleagues, Debra. I had been working with her team, and the communication just kept getting worse and worse until it was down to almost nothing. I used one of our tools, The Strategy Circle®, to get clear on the result I wanted, and then I showed it to another colleague, Ross, for his input. That was the smartest thing I could have done. He immediately noticed that I had missed the major issue. He pointed out that although I thought I had been treating them as equals, they didn't see *me* that way. I was a team leader, so they interpreted my requests as being bossy and demanding—not my intent at all!

With that knowledge, I had a meeting with Debra and expressed my appreciation for everything she and her team did, and my commitment to changing my behavior in whatever way I needed so we could have a strong working relationship. That expression of appreciation and commitment changed everything. From that point forward, we worked together well, with no issues. It was almost as though it had never happened.

What I learned is that my perspective—that we were all equals working on the same team—wasn't the same as everyone else's perspective. Until I understood where they were coming from, I couldn't bridge the gap. I'm now much more sensitive to how I'll be perceived, and I know that people don't just see me as Shannon the person, they also respond to my role in the company. I've never been particularly status-oriented, so I didn't get it. It's a lesson I've never forgotten.

Rugged Individualism.

One of the changes entrepreneurs, and even team members, have to make when they're growing the company is to stop being "Rugged Individualists." A Rugged Individualist believes, "I can do it better myself." While in certain cases, this is true (for example, when they're using their Unique Ability), it's not true all the time, or even most of the time.

However, it can take time to change behaviors, which get entrenched and become habits.

We get used to doing things our way, and when there are other team members asking us to do things differently, it's very easy to resist and resent them.

If you've ever worked with someone who didn't get to or hated certain activities but refused to give them up, then you know what I mean.

I frequently tease our clients about the death grip they have on certain tasks. Even though they don't like doing them, they're loath to give them up. Why? It's a habit. They're worried because they haven't communicated their standards and, as a result, they're not confident you'll do it as well.

This is a coaching opportunity. Using the guidelines from Strategies #3 and #9, you can start a conversation with the following: "I'd like to take this off your plate. What do I need to know so I can do it to your standards?"

By the way, this works for something as small as minor paperwork to taking over whole departments.

I learned this early on when working with Babs. Until I could describe the situation from her perspective—the result she was looking for and what she was worried about—she'd never hand over the project. When I did get it and could reflect it back to her, it was all mine. She had complete confidence. It was interesting to learn that it wasn't my brilliant answers and solutions that made her confident in delegating, but rather my understanding. And that made all the difference.

Delegation is hard. It takes trust and communication for it to work well, and few people take the time to set up the expectations and communication to make it a success.

Without delegation, though, we're never going to grow, and we're never going to be freed up to take on new and bigger challenges.

The goal, ultimately, is to build a Unique Ability® Team where everyone is playing to their strengths and doing what they love in service of a meaningful purpose and enjoying the rewards of a productive, happy, and profitable enterprise.

Take Action!
- Recognize that other people see the situation differently. Seek first to understand.
- Analyze what you're doing and be willing to let go of those things you don't truly enjoy.
- When you hand them off to others, let them know the final result you're looking for and your criteria for success.
- Know that it takes time to change entrenched habits and behaviors, and focus on "progress, not perfection."

Success Strategy #12: Don't give up.
Learn to see mistakes and breakdowns as learning opportunities.

Persevere.

The ability to overcome adversity is essential for any successful entrepreneur and entrepreneurial team member. It takes humility, and the willingness to be wrong, to not know, and to learn in order to ultimately be successful.

History is full of examples of entrepreneurs who failed not once but several times before they were successful: Henry Ford went bankrupt before he founded the Ford Motor Company and changed the course of human transportation.

Walt Disney was fired from his first job because "he lacked imagination and had no good ideas," and went bankrupt several times before he built Disneyland. Donald Trump, H.J. Heinz, George Foreman, and Milton Hershey all went bankrupt before they went on to experience success, and the list goes on.[9]

While it's likely not necessary for you to demonstrate this kind of resilience and perseverance, it is vital that you don't get too discouraged by mistakes and breakdowns.

Entrepreneurial undertakings always entail risk, venturing into the unknown, and experimenting with new approaches. It's natural, and to be expected, that it's not always going to go

9 For more information, visit
   http://www.incomediary.com/went-bankrupt-now-worth-millions

right the first time. How you respond is up to you.

It's not just the business's missteps that you want to learn from, but also your own. I've learned just as much or more from my failures as I have from my successes. I've finally come to see them all as learning adventures.

Is there a cost to making mistakes? Absolutely. Sometimes it's a blow to our ego; other times it costs us time and money. One of my clients calls it a "learning tax."

Dan makes a great point too: You're either on the winning team or the learning team.

How to get smarter.

We have a learning process that we use at Coach and in the Program when something doesn't go well to quickly get past our initial negativity and move forward to capture the learning.

First of all, we identify the situation we want to improve and learn from. We keep it brief, being careful to stick to the facts. Perhaps we missed a deadline or left out a step. Whatever it was, we write it down.

Then we identify what worked about the situation. We've learned that even when there are mistakes and breakdowns, it's not all bad. Acknowledging what did work re-establishes our confidence.

After that, we analyze what didn't work. This isn't about

playing the blame game. It's about each person honestly identifying where the ball got dropped, where there was a miscommunication, whatever the problem was. Dan has always said that 90 percent of the time, it's not a person at fault, it's the system.

This means we're always looking for what went wrong in our system, and not to blame an individual person. What's interesting is that this approach frees people to take responsibility when they've dropped the ball. They know that the team isn't looking for a scapegoat; they're looking for ways to help people be successful.

Then it's time to get creative. We brainstorm, asking ourselves, "Knowing what we know now, what would we do differently next time?" I love this part because of the insights and ideas that come out that are so different from mine. It's always a richer conversation when we're doing it as a team.

Finally, we take the best idea from our brainstorming and come up with a set of strategies that will keep what worked and prevent what didn't work from recurring. It's a fabulous debriefing tool after a meeting or an event. It's even useful to do it on a specific time frame like the previous quarter or the previous week—any circumstance you want to improve and learn from. I've even done it with my husband on a trip to Hawaii that did not go as planned!

Take Action!
- Always look for the lesson.
- Have a sense of humor.
- Be willing to learn—think through things that go wrong and get smarter for next time.

Conclusion

Thank you for reading! I'm excited for your future and grateful for the work you do every day that creates value for others.

My desire is that you accomplish your goals, grow as a person and as a team member, and maximize your contribution and your success.

I'd love to hear your stories and get your feedback. Please visit *yourteamsuccess.com* to share your comments.

Thank you!

About Strategic Coach®

The Strategic Coach Program, founded in 1989 by Dan Sullivan and Babs Smith, was the first coaching program exclusively for entrepreneurs and remains the most innovative in terms of its ability to help participants make successive quantum leaps toward increasingly greater personal and professional goals.

Strategic Coach clients today not only significantly increase their income and free time, they build strong, future-focused companies that leave their competition behind. Many have set new standards in their industries and made significant contributions to their communities through the increased focus, resources, and creativity gained by participating in the Program.

The Strategic Coach Inc.

Strategic Coach is an organization created by entrepreneurs, for entrepreneurs, and operates using the same philosophy, tools, and concepts taught in The Strategic Coach Program. With over 100 entrepreneurially-minded team members and four offices—Toronto, Chicago, Los Angeles, and the UK—the company continues to grow and enrich its offerings to an expanding global client base. Currently, over 3,000 successful and highly motivated entrepreneurs from over 60 industries and a dozen countries attend Strategic Coach workshops on a quarterly basis.

If you would like more information about Strategic Coach, its programs for entrepreneurs at all levels of success, or its many products for entrepreneurial thinkers, please call 416.531.7399 or 1.800.387.3206. Or visit *www.strategiccoach.com*.

About The Strategic Coach® Team Programs

At Strategic Coach, we know that building a team is crucial to the development of a Self-Managing Company®. In addition to The Strategic Coach Program, which is designed specifically for entrepreneurs, we offer a variety of programs to give our clients' team members first-hand experience learning the tools and strategies to better serve their companies.

A Strategic Assistant® is an entrepreneur's first and last line of defense against endless distractions, interruptions, and demands. **The Strategic Assistant® Webinar Program** gives assistants the knowledge and tools to help better focus their entrepreneur's time, activities, and relationships—so they can make constant progress toward their bigger future.

Team Tools® is a two-day workshop for team members where they'll learn how to use The Strategic Coach Program's entrepreneurial thinking tools to deliver great results on key projects; understand, communicate, and work more strategically; and have a personal stake in developing themselves within their role.

Designed to give the entire team the Strategic Coach experience, our **Onsite Advantage™** workshops are one-day workshops where we come to you! The goal of these workshops is to focus on the company's goals and the essential tools and concepts needed to reach them.

For more information about the Strategic Coach Team Programs, call 1.800.387.3206 in Canada or 1.888.872.8877 in the U.S. You can also email teamprograms@strategiccoach.com.

Note: The Strategic Coach Team Programs are available only to current participants in The Strategic Coach Program and their teams.

Acknowledgments

All books are a team effort, and this book is certainly no exception.

To my early readers and colleagues, Ben, Cathy, Julia, and Catherine, I cannot tell you how much confidence your positive feedback and creative direction gave me. This book is infinitely better because of your contributions.

Ben Lall—I love working with you! Our conversations about culture, value, teams, teamwork, and spirituality always inspire me. You're a gift in my life.

Cathy Davis—You're my creative partner and biggest fan, without whom NOTHING gets done. You're on my Positive Focus a lot. I'm blessed to have you in my life and can't imagine life without you. Don't ever leave me!

Catherine Nomura—You are my creative writing partner, colleague, and beautiful and talented friend. You've always been my champion, and my creative midwife, for which I'm eternally grateful. Your confidence in me inspires me. Thank you.

Kim White—You're a blessing in my life. As my friend and energy coach, you keep me clear, you free me up to always come from my heart, and you've supported me every step of the way. Thank you for sharing yourself and your gift with me.

To my dear lifelong friend and past colleague and Team Program coach, Ross Slater—The Entrepreneurial Attitude exercise came out of my experience in the workshops and conversations with you about what was missing. Thank you for your creative partnership and friendship over the years. I'm looking forward to many, many more.

None of this would have happened without getting to talk with some of my very favorite people—entrepreneurial team members. I love hearing what's working for you, what you're struggling with, and where you want to go. Thank you for all your insights, your coaching, and for listening. A special thanks to Diann Howard and Sandra Wiley, both extremely important people to their organizations who started in the original Strategic Assistant® Program in 1995. It's an honor to be your coach.

To my entrepreneur friends and clients, thank you for our in-depth conversations and for trusting me with your teams! I learn so much from hearing your issues. Thank you for your openness and partnership.

To our fabulous, intelligent, talented Team Program and teleseminar coaches and support team—Kristi Chambers, Maureen Sullivan Garrelts, Paulette Sopoci, Tanya Voytovech, Rebecca Powsney, and Marilyn Prebul—you deliver this content with grace, humor, and deep capability every time you coach.

Kathy Valant—You love the Team Programs, and it's evident every time you talk with clients about registering their teams.

In fact, you can't understand why someone wouldn't want to send their team members. Thank you for your devotion, for your partnership, and for filling the workshops so we get to do what we love to do.

Jodette Janowiak—You've been my faithful supporter from the beginning, and I deeply appreciate your partnership and between-session coaching of the Team Program participants. You love team members as much as I do. Thank you for changing people's lives for the better.

Marilyn Waller—Not only are you my mom, you're also my partner when working with teams because of your incredible insight and wisdom about people. Thank you for always trusting and supporting me. (Yes, I know you're also my biggest fan!)

Julia Waller—You've always supported me, and I've learned so much about teamwork from working with you. I've benefited from your amazing talents and from your Unique Ability coaching. Thank you and I love you.

Sue Fletcher—Thank you for making Dad happy. The two of you have always inspired me as great examples of teamwork and partnership.

To my Strategic Coach coaches and colleagues, past and present—I LOVE coming to work every day, in large part because of who I get to hang out with. Thank you for being my friends, for contributing your talents, and for being a

Unique Ability Team. I know this stuff works because you put it into practice every day.

To my delicious family—Bruce, you frequently hold down the fort so that I can travel for work, and Madison and Charlotte, you light up my life with your spirits and love. Thank you, thank you.

And, finally, to Dan and Babs.

Dan, thank you for always innovating and integrating—your insight never fails to amaze and inspire me. I ride on your coattails.

Babs, without you, there would be no team. It's your vision, your heart, and your trust that have created the most phenomenal work environment I know of. We're all free to be ourselves, learn, grow, and fulfill a vision of improving entrepreneurs' lives and those they impact. Thank you for being you. You're a special person, and I'm incredibly blessed to have you in my life.

With deepest gratitude.

The Entrepreneurial Attitude

Name: Date:

Definition

Jean-Baptiste Say, a French economist, is believed to have coined the word "entrepreneur" in the 19th century. He defined an entrepreneur as one who "shifts economic resources out of an area of lower and into an area of higher productivity and greater yield."

	Success Strategy	Description	Rating				
1	**Create value.**	Always work to provide leadership (direction), relationship (confidence), and creativity (capabilities).	Never 1	2	3	4	Always 5
2	**Take initiative.**	Look for ways to be proactive — solve problems, make improvements, and propose ideas.	Never 1	2	3	4	Always 5
3	**Focus on results.**	Focus on the bigger picture and the desired result, not just the time and effort required.	Never 1	2	3	4	Always 5
4	**Have an ownership attitude.**	Take full responsibility for your projects, your communication, and your actions.	Never 1	2	3	4	Always 5
5	**Be in alignment.**	Find out the overall goal or desired result and do what you need to do to align with it.	Never 1	2	3	4	Always 5
6	**Be a partner.**	Value and respect others' talents and goals as well as your own.	Never 1	2	3	4	Always 5
7	**Take action.**	Whenever possible, make things happen. Don't wait for others to make the first move.	Never 1	2	3	4	Always 5
8	**Be open.**	Be receptive to new ideas and initiatives. Prepare and plan for change.	Never 1	2	3	4	Always 5
9	**Communicate.**	Close "open files": Let people know when something is done and what happened. Prompt others to move projects ahead.	Never 1	2	3	4	Always 5
10	**Learn how to handle strong emotions.**	Have confidence and stay calm when dealing with emotionally-charged situations. These are a normal part of entrepreneurial life.	Never 1	2	3	4	Always 5
11	**Have patience and compassion.**	Look at the situation from the other person's point of view. Recognize that it takes time to change habits.	Never 1	2	3	4	Always 5
12	**Don't give up.**	Learn to see mistakes and breakdowns as learning opportunities.	Never 1	2	3	4	Always 5

Go to *yourteamsuccess.com* for a printable version of this exercise.

The 12 Strategies

	Success Strategy	Description
1	Create value.	Always work to provide leadership (direction), relationship (confidence), and creativity (capability).
2	Take initiative.	Look for ways to be proactive—solve problems, make improvements, and propose ideas.
3	Focus on results.	Focus on the bigger picture and the desired result, not just the time and effort required.
4	Have an ownership attitude.	Take full responsibility for your projects, your communication, and your actions.
5	Be in alignment.	Find out the overall goal or desired result, and do what you need to do to align with it.
6	Be a partner.	Value and respect others' talents and goals as well as your own.
7	Take action.	Whenever possible, make things happen. Don't wait for others to make the first move.
8	Be open.	Be receptive to new ideas and initiatives. Prepare and plan for change.
9	Communicate.	Learn how others like to communicate. Close "open files" — let people know when tasks are done and what happened.
10	Learn how to handle strong emotions.	Have confidence and stay calm when dealing with emotionally-charged situations. These are a normal part of entrepreneurial life.
11	Have patience and compassion.	Look at the situation from the other person's point of view. Recognize that it takes time to change habits.
12	Don't give up.	Learn to see mistakes and breakdowns as learning opportunities.

The Communication Builder

Name: Date:

1 Receiving Information	What's the most effective way to communicate with you?	What's the least effective way to communicate with you?
• Face to face • Bottom line • Phone • Lots of detail • Email • Lists • Voicemail • Diagrams/pictures • Text • Models		

2 Giving Information	What's your favorite way of giving information?	What's your least favorite way of giving information?
• Face to face • Bottom line • Phone • Lots of detail • Email • Lists • Voicemail • Diagrams/pictures • Text • Models		

3 Timing	When is the best time to communicate with you?	When is the worst time to communicate with you?
• Time of day • Last minute • In advance • Scheduled meetings • On the fly		

4 Handling Stress	What do you need to feel best supported?	What is the least effective way to support you?
• Focus time • Input from others • Reassurance • Time alone • Update meetings		

5 What is your biggest insight from doing this exercise?	6 What action can you take to improve your communication?

Go to *yourteamsuccess.com* for a printable version of this exercise.

The Positive Focus®

Name: Date:

	Achievement	Reason Why	Further Progress	First Action
1				
2				
3				
4				
5				

Go to *yourteamsuccess.com* for a printable version of this exercise.

Recommended Reading

Business Wisdom

 Radical Relevance: Sharpen Your Marketing Message – Cut Through the Noise – Win More Ideal Clients by Bill Cates

 Selling Boldly: Applying the New Science of Positive Psychology to Dramatically Increase Your Confidence, Happiness, and Sales by Alex Goldfayn

 The Success Lie: 5 Simple Truths to Overcome Overwhelm and Achieve Peace of Mind by Janelle Bruland

 Rocket Fuel: The One Essential Combination That Will Get You More of What You Want from Your Business by Gino Wickman and Mark C. Winters

 Business is Business: Reality Checks for Family-Owned Companies by Kathy Kolbe and Amy Bruske

 No Ego: How Leaders Can Cut Cost of Workplace Drama, End Entitlement, and Drive Big Results by Cy Wakeman

 Reality-Based Leadership: Ditch the Drama, Restore Sanity to the Workplace, and Turn Excuses Into Results by Cy Wakeman

 The Reality-Based Rules of the Workplace: Know What Boosts Your Value, Kills Your Chances, and Will Make You Happier by Cy Wakeman

🎙 Author Interview Podcast can be found on *yourteamsuccess.com*

Mr. Shmooze by Richard Abraham

 Business Brilliant: Surprising Lessons from the Greatest Self-Made Business Leaders about How to Build Wealth, Manage Your Career, and Take Risks by Lewis Schiff

 Polarity Management: Identifying and Managing Unsolvable Problems by Barry Johnson, Ph.D.

 Hug Your Customers: The Proven Way to Personalize Sales and Achieve Astounding Results by Jack Mitchell

A Complaint is a Gift: Using Customer Feedback as a Strategic Tool by Janelle Barlow and Claus Moller

Onward: How Starbucks Fought for Its Life without Losing Its Soul by Howard Schultz with Joanne Gordon

Do the Work by Steven Pressfield

Made to Stick: Why Some Ideas Survive and Others Die by Chip Heath and Dan Heath

Never Eat Alone And Other Secrets to Success, One Relationship at a Time by Keith Ferrazzi & Tahl Raz

Peak: How Great Companies Get Their Mojo from Maslow by Chip Conley

The Checklist Manifesto: How to Get Things Right by Atul Gawande

Fish! A Proven Way to Boost Morale and Improve Results by Stephen C. Lundin, Harry Paul, John Christensen, and Ken Blanchard

A Whole New Mind: Why Right-Brainers Will Rule the Future by Daniel H. Pink

How The Best Get Better® by Dan Sullivan

How the Best Get Better® 2 by Dan Sullivan

Ambition Series by Dan Sullivan

The End of Average: How We Succeed in a World That Values Sameness by Todd Rose

The Coaching Habit by Michael Bungay Stanier

Discovering Your Strengths
The Conative Connection: Uncovering the Link Between Who You Are and How You Perform by Kathy Kolbe

Strengths-Based Leadership: Great Leaders, Teams, and Why People Follow by Tom Rath and Barry Conchie

StandOut: The Groundbreaking New Strengths Assessment from the Leader of the Strengths Revolution by Marcus Buckingham

Unique Ability® 2.0: Discovery by Catherine Nomura, Julia Waller, and Shannon Waller

Communication

Connected Parenting: How to Raise a Great Kid
by Jennifer Kolari

Never Split The Difference: Negotiating As If Your Life Depended On It by Chris Voss

Fierce Conversations: Achieving Success at Work and in Life, One Conversation at a Time by Susan Scott

Just Listen: Discover the Secret to Getting Through to Absolutely Anyone by Mark Goulston

Personal Change

Soul Sense: Your Breakthrough to Soul-Full Living and Leadership by Adrienne Duffy

Indistractable: How to Control Your Attention and Choose Your Life by Nir Eyal

Atomic Habits: An Easy & Proven Way to Build Good Habits & Break Bad Ones by James Clear

The Miracle Morning: The 6 Habits that Will Transform Your Life Before 8 a.m. by Hal Elrod

The Miracle Morning for Addiction Recovery: Letting Go of Who You've Been for Who You Can Become by Hal Elrod, Anna David, Joe Polish & Honoree Corder

The Surrender Experiment: My Journey into Life's Perfection by Michael A. Singer

The Untethered Soul: The Journey Beyond Yourself
by Michael A. Singer

The Life-Changing Magic of Tidying Up: The Japanese Art of Decluttering and Organizing by Marie Kondo

 Necessary Endings: The Employees, Businesses, and Relationships That All of Us Have to Give Up in Order to Move Forward by Dr. Henry Cloud

The Happiness Advantage: The Seven Principles Of Positive Psychology That Fuel Success And Performance At Work by Shawn Achor

 One Small Step Can Change Your Life: The Kaizen Way by Robert Maurer, Ph.D.

Driven To Distraction by Edward M. Hallowell & John J. Ratey

 Less Doing, More Living: Make Everything in Life Easier by Ari Meisel

Mindset: The New Psychology of Success by Carol S. Dweck, Ph. D.

 The Power of TED by David Emerald

The Gap And The Gain by Dan Sullivan

Teamwork And Culture

The Collaborative Way: A Story about Engaging the Mind and Spirit of a Company by Lloyd Fickett & Jason Fickett

The Ideal Team Player: How to Recognize and Cultivate The Three Essential Virtues by Patrick M. Lencioni

Hug Your People: The Proven Way to Hire, Inspire, and Recognize Your Employees and Achieve Remarkable Results by Jack Mitchell

Tribal Leadership: Leveraging Natural Groups to Build a Thriving Organization by Dave Logan, John King & Haylee Fischer-Wright

Delivering Happiness: A Path to Profits, Passion and Purpose by Tony Hsieh

The Five Dysfunctions of a Team: A Leadership Fable by Patrick Lencioni

Overcoming The Five Dysfunctions of a Team: A Field Guide for Leaders, Managers, and Facilitators by Patrick Lencioni

Death by Meeting: A Leadership Fable...About Solving the Most Painful Problem in Business by Patrick Lencioni

Getting Naked: A Business Fable About Shedding the Three Fears That Sabotage Client Loyalty by Patrick Lencioni

The Advantage: Why Organizational Health Trumps Everything Else in Business by Patrick Lencioni

Shannon Waller is a passionate expert on entrepreneurial teams. With Strategic Coach® since 1991, she's the creator of The Entrepreneurial Team® Program, a parallel program for team members of Coach clients that focuses on fostering a winning Entrepreneurial Attitude in its participants.

A key decision-maker at Strategic Coach and a recognized entrepreneurial team expert, Shannon is a sought-after speaker, presenter, and coach. She's a Kolbe Certified™ Consultant, and the 2015 recipient of the Kolbe Professional Award for individual leadership in building conative excellence. In addition to *The Team Success Handbook*, she is also author of *Multiplication By Subtraction*, a comprehensive guide to gracefully letting go of wrong-fit team members, and co-author of the bestselling book *Unique Ability® 2.0: Discovery*.

Made in the USA
Middletown, DE
25 October 2022